KIDS' ROOMS

KIDS' ROOMS

Imaginative Ideas for Creating the Perfect Space for Your Child

by Jack Maguire

HPBooks

HPBooks, Inc.
P.O. Box 5367
Tucson, AZ 85703
(602) 888-2150

Publisher: Rick Bailey
Executive Editor: Randy Summerlin

ISBN: 0-89586-500-9 (hardcover)
0-89586-524-6 (paperback)

Library of Congress Catalog Card Number: 86-82120

KIDS' ROOMS: Imaginative Ideas for Creating the Perfect Space for Your Child
was prepared and produced by
Quarto Marketing Ltd.
15 West 26th Street
New York, NY 10010

Editor: Pamela Hoenig
Art Director: Mary Moriarty
Designer: Liz Trovato
Photo Editor: Susan M. Duane
Photo Research: Sherry Gilligan
Production Manager: Karen L. Greenberg

Typeset by B.P.E. Graphics
Color separations by South Seas Graphic Art Company
Printed and bound in Hong Kong by Leefung-Asco Printers Ltd.

Dedication

To my niece, Mandy Maguire, and my nephew, Chad Maguire.

Acknowledgments

I'm indebted to the many designers
who volunteered ideas out of a sheer love for children
and to my editor, Pam Hoenig, for bringing this project together.

CONTENTS

Introduction
Page 9

Introduction

Close your eyes and summon up images of the room you had when you were a child. Maybe you remember a cozy rocking chair that was just your size, or a handcrafted wooden toy chest that was wonderful to smell and touch, or a fanciful parade of dancing letters and numbers winding across the walls, just below the ceiling.

A child's memories center on the room (or rooms) that he or she occupies. As parents, you want to give your child living, learning, playing and sleeping space that will enrich those memories in addition to being safe, accessible and easy to maintain.

Kids' Rooms helps you to plan and furnish a bedroom or playroom that is both attractive and practical: one that appeals to your child's imagination as well as makes design sense. The book offers guidelines for utilizing room space effectively, creating wall, ceiling and floor treatments that are functional and fun, and buying or building furniture and room accessories that are durable and attractive. It tells you how to set up a room that will accommodate the changing needs of your child as he or she moves from childhood to adolescence. It also contains easy-to-follow, step-by-step directions for constructing specific projects by yourself.

Kids' Rooms emphasizes how to provide a room for your child that exhibits good design qualities. A visually appealing, well-made environment will not only motivate your child to take care of it and use it productively, it will also heighten your child's imagination and awareness of form and style.

CHAPTER 1

Planning and Creating a Kid's Room

kid's room has many functions. It's an amusement park, a laboratory, a workshop, a study hall, a fitness center, a hospital, a social club, a warehouse, a theater for dreams. It also undergoes periodic transformation: from the early fuzzy-bear-and-balloon stage, through the playhouse-and-craft years, into the age of pennants, posters and stereos.

Putting together a comfortable and attractive kid's room that takes into account all the possible evolutions during the growing-up process is a stimulating and rewarding challenge. Designing a room is an opportunity for each member of the household to apply personal ingenuity toward projects that are both eminently practical and visually pleasing.

A kid's room needs to be reviewed and probably redecorated at least three times during the child's life at home: at the beginning of the preschool, "toddler" stage of development (when your child is 2 to 3 years old), during the onset of the school years (when your child is 4 to 6 years old) and around the time your child becomes what is known as a teenager (which can be anywhere from 10 to 13 years old, depending on his or her physical and emotional rate of growth). When-

In a bedroom shared by two sisters—a toddler and a grade-schooler—space is carefully allotted and designed so that each sister can enjoy both her personal territory and the room as a whole. Fake ceiling beams and a stenciled floor design lend ageless charm and unity.

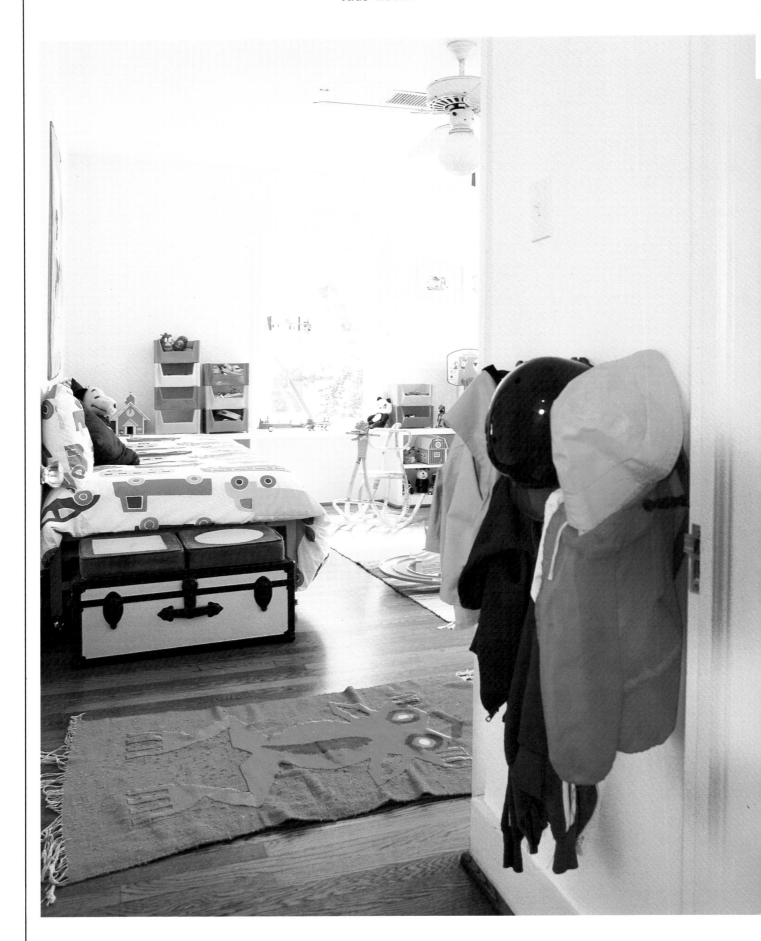

ever you and your child decide the room needs a major remodeling, divide your planning into two broad areas: first, consider the space itself and second, the contents that will fill the space, which include all the furnishings as well as wall, floor and ceiling treatments.

In terms of space, the preschooler needs a lot of room for spontaneous physical activity, so the floor should be kept as clear of unnecessary furnishing obstacles as possible. The school-age child becomes more and more oriented toward specific tasks that require functional furniture. As a result, as the child grows older floor space becomes less important. This trend continues into the teenage years.

Space in a kid's room should be organized according to the different functions it needs to serve. Assigning separate areas for sleeping, dressing, playing and studying allows for maximum effectiveness in conducting each of these activities, and it gives the room an overall neat and orderly appearance.

If the room is being shared by more than one child, it's important not only to save space but also to devise ways of defining each child's personal territory. Among other things, you'll want to reserve at least one particular area, such as a corner or a closet, to be each child's "private" spot.

A primary factor in planning any kid's room is ensuring good health and safety. Make certain the space is properly

Above: **The odd proportions of this room for two school-aged boys are relieved by the clever arrangement of space and the repeated use of a square motif. Colorful spreads make each bed a separate focal point against a neutral background.**

Facing page: **An all white paint scheme enables you to make liberal use of colors in the furnishings and contents of a child's bedroom. Here a rainbow assortment of plastic drawer modules makes for tough, portable and efficient toy storage. Even a loaded clothes rack succeeds in being attractive as well as practical.**

heated and ventilated. Check window sashes, doorways, electrical outlets, radiators, exposed pipes and closet interiors with an eye for possible hazards. Envision likely traffic patterns and set up any activity-specific areas in the room so that these patterns are not liable to invite unwanted accidents.

The contents of a kid's room will have to stand a lot of rough use. Furnishings must be durable, easy to clean and not likely to cause injury (which means, for example, avoiding rugs that slide easily or furniture that has sharp angles). If your child is very young, you may want to incorporate a drawing board or chalkboard into your wall treatment to keep him or her from scribbling directly onto painted or papered walls. If two or more children share a room, you may want to divide the room with supergraphics on the wall or differently colored carpets on the floor.

Color is a vital tool in designing a successful child's room. Do you want to make the room look larger? Use soft, light colors on the walls or a paper with a small print. Do you want the room to look smaller? Use bold, vibrant tones on the walls or a paper with a large print. Warmer? Use reds, oranges, yellows and emerald greens. Cooler? Use dark greens, blues, grays and purples. An ideal way to enliven the room and at the same time stimulate your child's creativity is to stencil a design or paint a mural across one or more wall surfaces.

The graceful white metalwork of this headboard stands out beautifully against a soothing gray-blue wall surface. By contrast, the quilted bed coverings, while echoing the lines of the headboard and the hue of the wall, offer a richly exuberant display of colors and patterns.

This bedroom is made cozy and personal by a child-sized chair and a detailed stencil design that runs along the wooden baseboards and trim. Notice how the stencil design is thematically tied to the wallpaper design. Both designs are repeated in the curtain border. The total effect is one of loving care and harmony.

The furniture in a child's room necessarily has a short lifetime. Children are so appreciative of furniture scaled to their size that you'll want to buy them some new pieces at different stages of their physical growth. This results in a relatively rapid turnover of kids' furniture compared to the furniture in the rest of the house. In addition, children wear out and change their tastes in furniture often. They occasionally pick up interests that require new pieces, such as a storage locker for a fledgling major-leaguer's sports equipment or an additional bookcase for an avid reader. For all these reasons, don't over-design a room so that it demands a large amount or a particular style of furniture. Furniture should be lightweight and easy to move so that your child can rearrange it to suit shifting moods and activities.

In a room shared by two or more children, the furniture can be color-coded to indicate

Facing page: A duck-shaped wicker rocking chair, colorful cushions and a delightful wall hanging lend graceful notes to this child's room, which consists mainly of utilitarian furniture lined against the wall to allow for maximum floor space.

Above: Toys can frequently perform double duty as decorative accents, like these dolls and stuffed animals sitting on top of playfully patterned bed linens.

Below: This storage wall in a bedroom for two girls features a separate color-coded shelf-and-drawer unit for each girl plus a printer's drawer and small wall-mounted shelf unit in between that they can share.

Facing page: A button-and-bows wallcovering is nicely complemented by a fabric with a tiny rose design, which was also used to make the curtains, pillowcases and duster. Many kids find such coordination pleasingly reassuring.

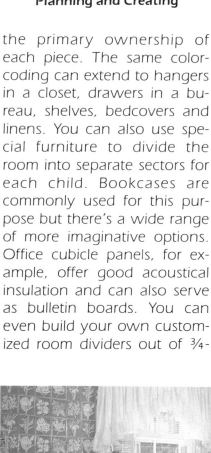

the primary ownership of each piece. The same color-coding can extend to hangers in a closet, drawers in a bureau, shelves, bedcovers and linens. You can also use special furniture to divide the room into separate sectors for each child. Bookcases are commonly used for this purpose but there's a wide range of more imaginative options. Office cubicle panels, for example, offer good acoustical insulation and can also serve as bulletin boards. You can even build your own customized room dividers out of ¾-inch plywood mounted on a wooden stand.

Your ultimate goal is to produce a room that pleases both you and your child. It shouldn't be a room that is cut off completely from the rest of the house, yet it should be a room that clearly belongs to your child. To create such a room, work in close cooperation with your child, selecting ideas that you like from specific examples offered in the following chapters and tailoring them to fit your special individual needs, visions and surroundings.

Photo: Bill Rothschild; Design: Classic Galleries/Peg Heron and Claudia Dowling

Left: **Boxes, baskets and even houses for storing toys and other assorted stuff fit nicely into a wall of modular shelves. These shelves are nicely counterbalanced by the size and design of the window on the adjoining wall.**

Above: **A bold and unusual floral pattern on the walls gives this somewhat formal room a playful feeling, emphasized by the presence of an ornate dollhouse and stuffed animals in one corner.**

Above: In a room filled with functional metal furnishings, a wall-mounted bicycle represents not only a practical storage solution but also an ingenious decorating strategy.

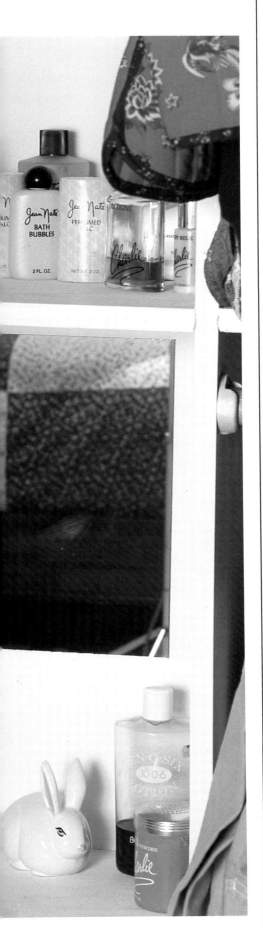

Above: A combination dollhouse and shelving unit includes pegs on the roof for holding hats.

Left: These two shelf cubicles take the place of the traditional vanity table. They are part of an easy-to-build pine structure that surrounds a clothes rack.

CHAPTER 2

Walls, Ceilings and Floors

No feature of your home gets more attention or physical abuse than the outer boundaries of your child's room.

Kids spend a major portion of their time on the floor of their room—playing, exercising, socializing, thinking, resting. Walls are continually used for drawing, supporting headstands, displaying personal treasures and halting airborne objects. And to people who are preoccupied with growing bigger and testing limits, the ceiling becomes an irresistible place to bounce balls, leap up and touch and attack with water pistols.

Even when kids aren't busy enjoying the functional aspects of their walls, ceilings or floors, they are often relishing the mere presence of these surfaces. They can ponder them for hours, letting their imaginations roam as they study the particular colors, patterns and textures spread out before them.

How the walls look is the major determinant of how the room looks as a whole. An all-white wall treatment may form the most compatible backdrop for an assortment of toys and furnishings in different hues, but it may not accommodate your child's love for color or give the kind of unique identity your child needs in his surroundings. A bold color or pattern splashed across all four walls is stimulating to your child's senses and sets the room clearly apart from the rest of the house. However, such boldness may

Above: A Noah's ark theme ties together the stencils on the wall and the bed. The windows have been carefully treated to avoid competing ornamentation.

Photo: © Boyce Graham; Design: Renée Ritter Graham, ASID

Below: The designs on these platform and cushion coverings have
been restated on the walls above,
making the entire corner look like a
sleek, built-in seating area.

Courtesy of Motif Designs

Photo: Karen Bussolini; Painting: John Canning

be difficult to live with over an extended period of time and will certainly limit the colors and patterns you can use within the room.

The solution is to aim for a balance of simple and dramatic elements in your wall design. Paint one wall with a vivid color or, better still, a mural, and paint the other walls with a softer, complementary color or all-purpose white. Another solution is to paper one wall with an exciting pattern, and then cover the other walls with a companion paper in a solid color.

An alternative is to keep all four walls fairly subdued and add enlivening details. Cut out or buy a rigid stencil depicting something that interests your child—a duck, an airplane or a flower—and create an eye-catching border around all four walls of the room. Paint a supergraphic, such as a thick arrow or rainbow-striped ribbon, that winds across walls, doors and even the ceiling.

In addition to having the most impact on the appearance of the room, the walls also bear the brunt of your child's active curiosity, so their coverings need to be durable and easy to clean and repair. If you decide to paint the walls, use latex or plastic-based paint, which can be washed with a sponge and is thin enough to allow for smooth touch-ups. Enamel paint has a nice shine and can also be

A large central floor space is rendered more intimate and inviting by a lovely, dancing pattern of over-sized thistles and flowers.

Above: The huge scale and unusual perspective of this mural spread across two walls and the ceiling help to make this box-shaped bed room for two seem larger and more dramatic, as does the use of a plat-form to create a two-level floor.

Facing page, top: Half window, half skylight, this opening into the out-door world compensates for the low slope of the ceiling.

Facing page, bottom: A stenciled border defines a space for storing shoes—for both dolls and real people.

sponge-cleaned, but because it is difficult to apply evenly, future touch-ups will be more visible. If the walls are fairly rough, you may prefer a dirt-resistant wallcovering such as treated paper, textured grass cloth or vinyl cloth. Laminated paneling, which requires less maintenance than paint or any other wallcovering, is an increasingly popular choice, especially for the rooms of younger children.

Kids from the ages of 2 to approximately 8 (when they begin to develop an awareness of property and propriety) love to mark on walls. With this in mind, you may want to attach a large chalkboard along the base of one wall. For maximum protection, you can install a wooden rail about 3 feet high along all 4 walls and put up plastic paneling below the rail. Children also like to hang things on walls, so look for clever ways to incorporate corkboards, pegboards and hardwood surfaces into your wall treatment. For young school-aged children, a 2- to 3-inch strip of plywood nailed or screwed along one or more walls approximately 4 feet above the floor makes a wonderful place to pin drawings or notes and, with the addition of pegs, to hang clothes, toys and sports equipment.

Ceilings, like walls, need to be easy to clean as well as pleasant to look at. In addition to painting or stenciling colorful designs directly onto the ceiling surface, you can use the ceiling for hanging mobiles, toys that spin, paper dec-

Courtesy of Velux-America, Inc.

orations or model airplanes. Older children may enjoy loud music, so you might want to line the ceiling (and some of the walls) with acoustical tile squares, which will effectively absorb sound.

Floors are best kept smooth and clear, especially for younger children. Wooden floors that have been well sanded and sealed with several coats of polyurethane provide beauty plus excellent traction for walking and playing with blocks and toys with wheels.

More important, they are simple to maintain, unlike carpeted floors, which hold onto stains, odors and dust despite frequent vacuuming. Vinyl, cushioned vinyl, cork or linoleum flooring combines practicality with the striking colors and patterns that kids like. Laying sheets or tiles of this kind of resilient flooring makes an ideal do-it-yourself project.

After the age of 8 your child is apt to be less messy, more oriented toward table-and-chair tasks and, as a result,

Facing page: An awkward nook in this child's bedroom is transformed into a ramp bordered by storage stairs. The charming mysteriousness of the place is enhanced by the skylight and the jigsaw-patterned wallpaper.

Below: In this bedroom, imagination has triumphed over awkward proportions. The rainbow colors in a kite hung across one wall are repeated in the breezy strokes on two of the other walls.

Photo: Lea Babcock; Design: Thomas Eickhoff

ready for wall-to-wall carpeting. The most appropriate choice is a flat, tightly woven, loop-pile carpet in a synthetic fabric, such as nylon or olefin. This type of carpet resists abrasion and stains and retains its color even after many years of use. A carpet featuring several intertwined shades of the same color hides dirt more successfully than any other style of carpet.

Many kids (and their parents) favor different floor coverings for various areas of the room. Young children may want a small, nonskid rug next to their bed or in a quiet corner underneath a few large pillows. Older children may welcome an attractive area rug, one they can move around or take with them when they eventually move away from home.

Whatever you do with the walls, ceilings and floors of your child's room, make sure that the materials involved will stay strong and fresh-looking for a long period of time. The "shell" of your child's room may change only once or twice in all the time he or she lives at home, while the contents may change every few months.

Courtesy of Levolor Lorentzen

Tim Street Porter/EWA

Above: The bedroom walls seem to disappear in this trompe d'oeil mural—an illusion that is reinforced by the framed print, a work of the surrealist Magritte.

Above: This simple-to-execute mural covers all surfaces of an apartment bedroom, bringing to it a spaciousness, charm and repose it would otherwise lack.

Facing page: This wonderfully complex mural teases the mind as well as the eye. It presents a magic gateway into an unreal world while concealing an ordinary door to a real closet.

Several elements combine to produce this peaceful, natural-style bedroom: subtly textured wallpaper and wood paneling; a chest of drawers and wooden wall-strip painted to match the trim on an interior window box; translucent curtains with a tiny floral print.

Painting a Mural

A wall mural is a uniquely warm and personal way to enliven a room and stretch your child's imagination. You don't have to be a professional artist to paint a mural or to achieve attractive results. The procedure described here involves using a simple grid technique to transfer any design from a piece of paper to an area of any size on a wall. An alternative is to trace a design from a slide projected directly onto the wall.

1. Trace or draw a design with clear outlines on a sheet of paper. Choose a design that will look good on the wall space you have selected for the mural. Children particularly like designs that tell (or imply) one or more stories. Consider designs that include your child's favorite storybook, cartoon, television or movie characters and objects.

2. Carefully draw a grid of squares across that design. Each square should be the same size— approximately ½ inch to 1 inch on a side.

3. With a pencil, lightly draw another grid of squares in the same shape with the same number of squares over the wall area you intend to paint.

4. Transfer the details that fill each square on your sheet of paper to the corresponding square on the wall, using the same pencil with a slightly darker stroke (not so dark that it will show through paint later on, but dark enough for the outline to be distinguishable from the grid itself).

5. Assemble the paint for the mural. You can use either latex or alkyd paints. Latex paints are water-based, which makes them odorless, quick-drying and easy to clean. Alkyd paints (such as high gloss and semi-gloss enamels) are more durable, come in a wider range of colors and offer a richer finish, but they require turpentine or some other chemical solvent for thinning and cleaning. Make sure you have a variety of brushes in different sizes that are appropriate for the paint you're using and lots of containers (such as cut-off milk cartons or coffee cans) for mixing and storing paints.

6. Working from the top of the mural to the bottom to avoid paint drips, paint all areas of a single color. Begin with the color that covers the most territory. Be sure to mix all the paint you will need of that color (plus some surplus paint for touch-ups) before you start, to ensure you won't have matching problems afterwards. Let each color dry before moving on to the next.

7. When the mural is finished and dry, paint over it with a thin coat of matt polyurethane varnish to heighten the colors. This will also make it easy to clean and protect it from staining and chipping.

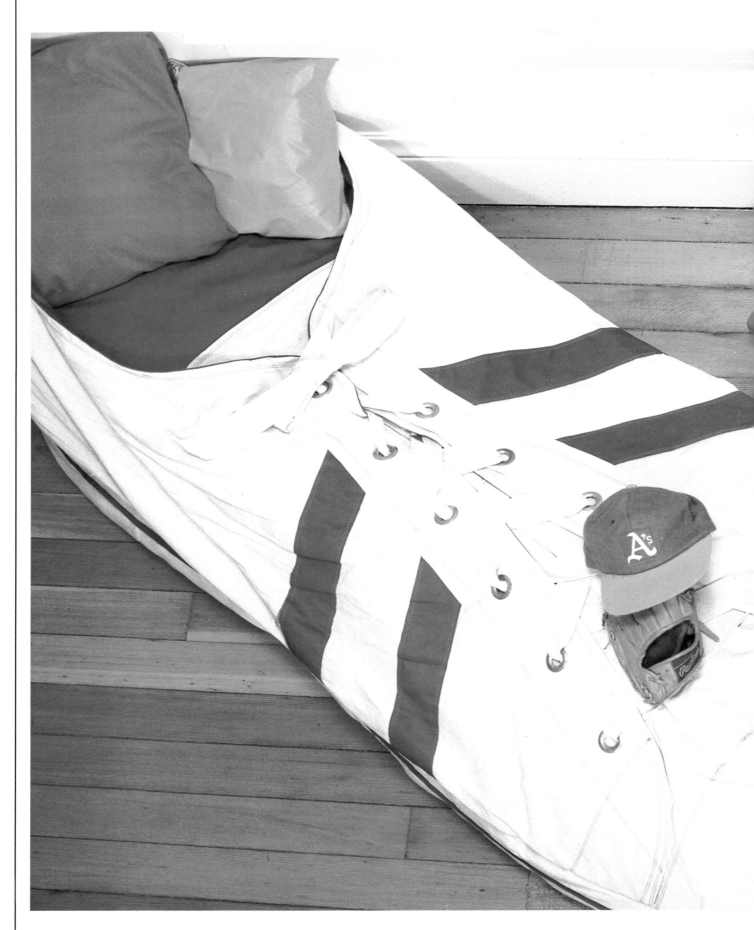

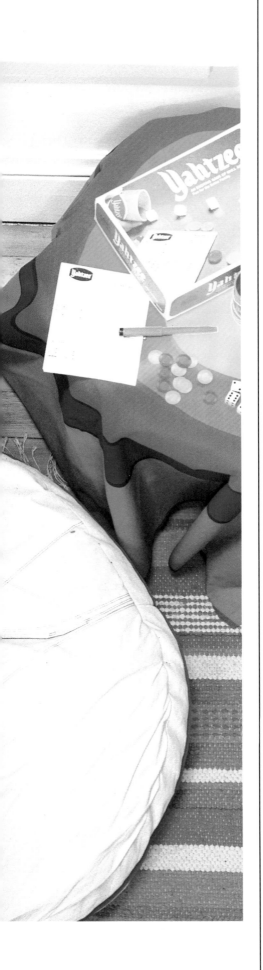

CHAPTER 3
Sweet Dreams

T he focal point of any bedroom is naturally the bed. But a child's room isn't just a bedroom, and a child's bed isn't just a bed. What seems to be a piece of furniture primarily designed for resting and sleeping can also serve as a clubhouse, a playground, a pirate ship, a hilltop, a woodland bower, a chuckwagon or a treasure trove. Because the bed is both the biggest, most versatile item in your child's room and the primary location of your child's creative activities, you need to give special consideration to its scale, structural properties and design elements.

Once your child is ready to move out of a crib, which usually happens sometime between the ages of 2 and 4, the first decision you will have to make is the most appropriate size for the bed. At this stage in their lives some children will be most comfortable with a youth bed or a junior bed, which takes up about three-quarters of the space of a standard twin bed. Not only does a youth bed leave more floor space available in the room for playing and for other furniture, but it also provides psychological reassurance to children who, like Goldilocks, crave things that are exactly their size. Other children will prefer a bed that is "grown-up" or that offers lots of stretching space. Because comfortable sleep is vital to the health of your child, it is well worth respecting his or her personal preference.

A closet area on one side and an extended corkboard wall on the other have been neatly designed to turn this elevated bed into a snug and personalized retreat. Double laddering provides visual interest, safety and a sturdy frame for play and exercise.

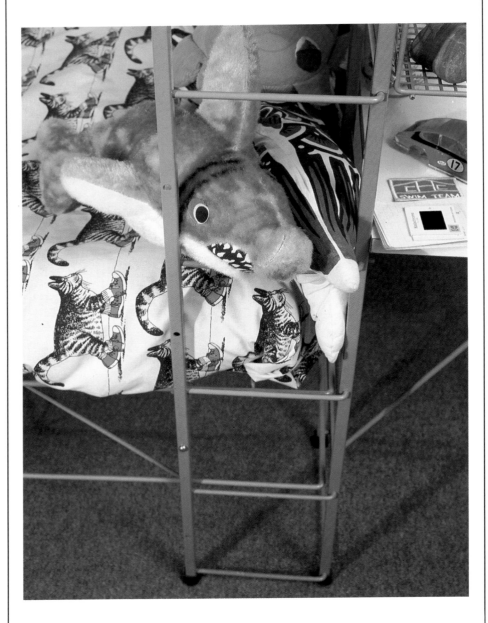

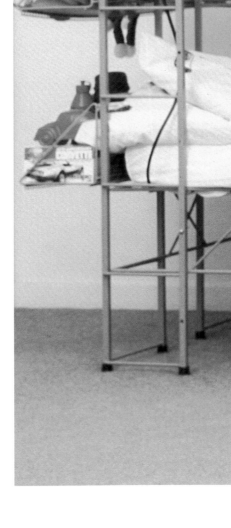

Right: This entire bed unit with attached shelves and a fold-down desk is extremely functional and yet has the abstract geometric beauty of a high-tech sculpture. *Above:* The ladder to the upper bunk is part of the structural support for the double-decker bed.

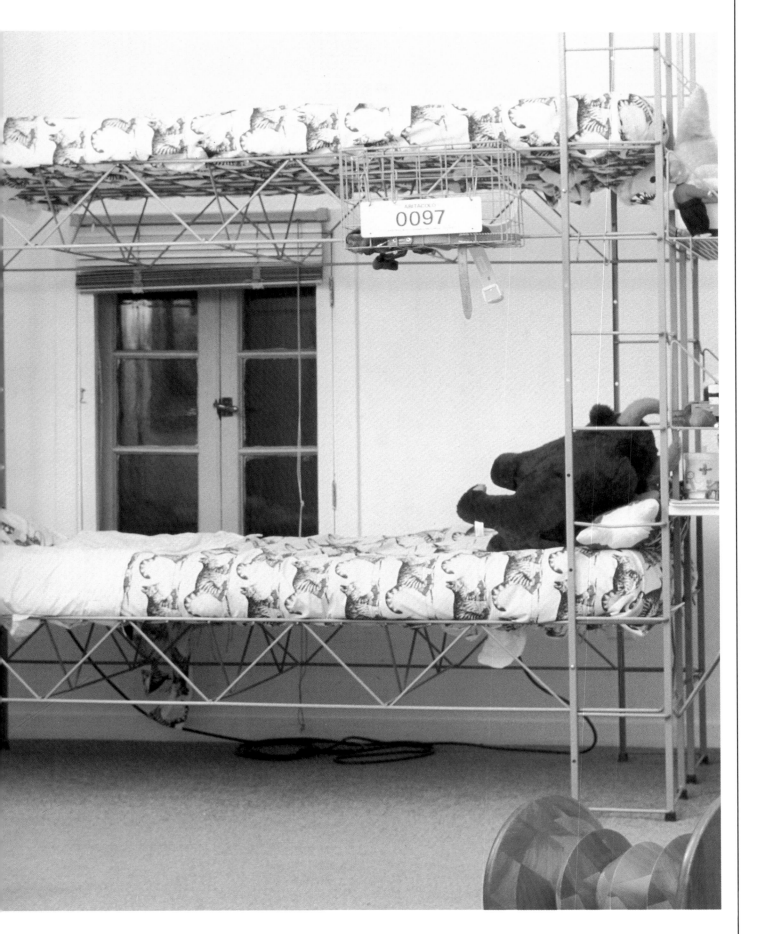

Photo: Robert Grant; Design: Albert Turick for Marimekko

Above: A slightly elevated bed, an adjoining portable staircase and a duffel bag for storage are boldly colored to coordinate with matching wallpaper and bed coverings. The result is a clean, vigorous and unified design.

Facing page: Two partially sheltered beds plus two separate floor levels offer plenty of opportunities for individual privacy in a small, oddly shaped room for twins.

There are other ways to save space in a room besides cutting down the size of the bed. The actual mattress-and-frame unit of your child's bed can be mounted on a platform that rests on top of a storage unit or that forms the ceiling of a play nook or small study area. Elevated beds can be very enticing to children, giving them a refreshingly lofty perspective on the world around them, but they also require extra attention to safety. Don't raise the mattress frame itself more than 2 feet off the floor unless your child is at least 6 years old—big enough and coordinated enough to negotiate a ladder easily. No matter how old your child is, there should be a guardrail around the mattress to prevent accidental falls.

Bunk beds are also popular with school-age children and come in two basic models: the classic two-decker and the more contemporary cornered construction, in which the lower bunk is set at a right angle to the upper one, creating interior space for a storage unit or table. Far from being strictly a space-saving solution in a room shared by two children, a bunk bed has a great deal of value in a room occupied by only one child. In this case, the additional bed can function as a play area, a storage platform or a bed for friends who stay overnight. Although a Murphy bed (one that folds into a vertical cabinet when not in use) is too cumbersome for a young child to operate on a day-to-day basis, it is ideal for guests or for a teenager whose room is small. Other options for the all-important guest sleeping space include a trundle bed or a futon, which can perform double-duty as a couch or daytime resting space.

When two children share a room, a bunk bed is not always the most desirable sleeping arrangement, especially when they reach their teen-age years. Kids of this age are more concerned with an outward show of equal treatment, and one child sleeping on the top bunk and the other on the bottom doesn't satisfy that concern. The only logical alternative is twin beds. To avoid a sterile and space-consuming "hotel room" look, each bed should be placed against a wall, so that the beds are either opposite each other or at right angles.

Any child's bed, whether it's a junior bed, an elevated bed, a bunk bed, a twin bed or a double bed, benefits from an imaginative design treatment—one that inspires the child's own creative play and makes the prospect of sleeping or resting all the more enjoyable. Some traditional bed styles have a built-in appeal to children: the canopied bed, which suggests a romantic retreat, or Early American beds with their handsomely carved head- and baseboards. Contemporary designers have produced some delightfully whimsical styles that cater directly to a child's active sense of wonder. Among the beds you can buy or build yourself are a sports car bed, a rocket ship bed, a circus wagon bed or a cloud bed, all of which consist simply of wooden attachments to a basic box-shaped bed frame.

You don't have to turn the bed as a whole into a fanciful work of art to give it charm and character. If the bed has a simple wooden headboard, try stenciling a design on it or cutting a circle or star through it. If it has no headboard, make one out of a single sheet of plywood that looks like a castle, a giant moon or a mountain range, or paint a false headboard on the wall behind the mattress. It takes only a little ingenuity to turn a dull and cumbersome piece of furniture into a dynamic centerpiece for the entire room.

Photo: Durston Saylor; Design: Gwen Jaffe

Facing page: There is plenty of easy-to-use storage space underneath this elevated bed. The building-block style drawer arrangement is pleasingly echoed in the stair construction, the mounted print and the cubic side table.

Above: Simple plywood cutouts transform this L-shaped elevated bed complex into a beautiful and inviting area for play, or sleep.

Facing page: An elegant brass bed sets the tone for this romantic bedroom. The less interesting bottom railings have been painted white for easy maintenance as well as for a softer, more restful effect.

Above: This elegant canopy bed is rendered more childlike and romantic by a hand-painted design on each bedpost that matches the fabric print.

Building an Elevated Bed

A cozy corner aerie for lounging and sleeping not only makes naptime and bedtime more enticing to children, but it also gives them extra space for storing their clothes and toys. The design presented here is easy to adapt. Simply allow the size of your junior-bed, bunk-bed or twin-bed mattress to determine the length and width of the unit as a whole. The finished product can be decorated with paint in any fashion that suits you and your child.

1. Cut three 5-foot-high rectangles from ¾-inch plywood that are 2 inches wider than the width of the mattress. One of these rectangles will support the head of the bed, one will support the foot of it and one will stand halfway between to divide the shelf area from the closet area below.

2. According to the dimensions you have created, cut 5 shelves, 2 doors and a platform from ¾-inch plywood to support the mattress.

3. Set the upright rectangles in place in a corner of your child's room and nail the mattress platform to the top of each rectangle using 3 evenly spaced 8-penny nails.

4. Support the mattress platform with short blocks of 1-by-3-inch ply-

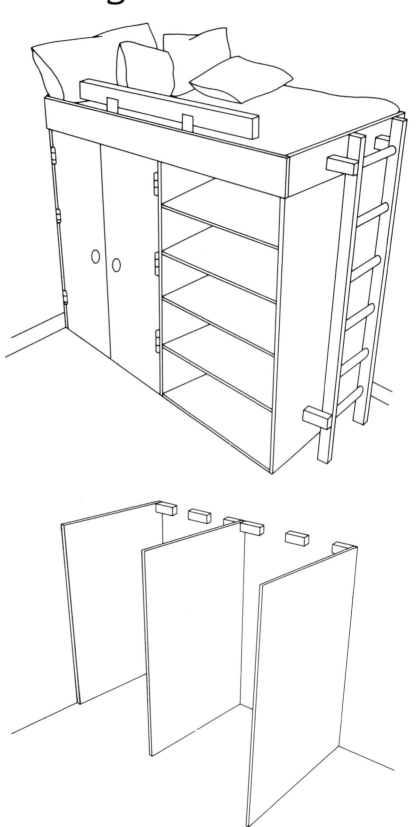

wood nailed to the studs in the wall.

5. Cut a 5-inch strip of 1-inch ply-wood that is long enough to form a barrier along the outside length of the mattress platform. Cut another 5-inch strip of 1-inch plywood that is long enough to form a barrier along the outside width of the mattress platform. Nail both strips flush to the edge of the mattress platform with 8-penny nails every few inches.

6. Mount a guardrail of 1-by-4-inch plywood approximately 4 feet long on 2 right-angle metal shelf supports placed 18 inches apart midway along the length of the mattress plat-form. Screw the supports into the mattress platform.

7. Make a ladder by nailing six 10-inch-long, evenly spaced, 1½-inch dowels to 1-by-3-inch plywood sides that are 5½ feet high. Mount the lad-der on the rectangular upright and barrier at the foot of the bed by using 4 blocks of 1-by-3-inch plywood about 5 inches long.

8. Secure 4 shelves in place with shelf brackets: 2 brackets to each side, with each bracket about 3 inches in from the nearest corner.

9. Nail knobs to the doors and mount them on hinges; 3 hinges to a door.

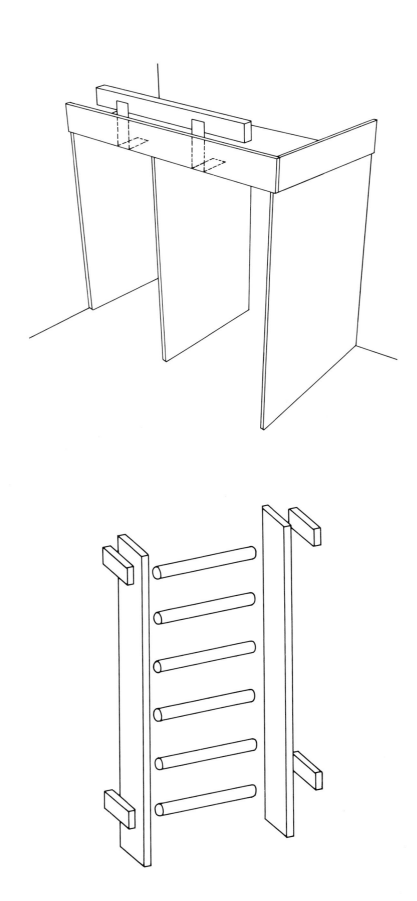

Photo: Daniel Eifert; Design: Rubén de Saavedra

CHAPTER 4
Play Spaces

lay is a child's work. Children instinctively rely on play to develop their bodies, sharpen their minds, discover their personal capabilities and interests, and learn about the social and physical world around them.

Because play contributes so much to a child's well-being, it makes sense to devote an entire room to play, especially if bedroom space is limited or you have more than one child. A playroom is, in fact, a child's "living" room. Unlike the bedroom, its main purpose is to provide an atmosphere that encourages creative entertainment, in addition to a place he or she can share on equal terms with a brother, a sister, a parent, a relative or a good friend.

The most valuable single feature of any child's playroom is open space that the child can fill, or not fill, as he or she sees fit. Keep the center of the room free of any furniture. Around the periphery of this open space (along the walls), establish various functional areas for different kinds of play. One area can be designed for physical exercise, with a mat, a hanging rope, a modular play structure or small weights. Another area, containing cars and trucks, dolls or a collapsible playhouse, can be reserved for social play. A third area can be equipped for table work: a spot to draw, mold clay, build models or engage in a hobby. A final area can be marked off as a "quiet place," complete with pillows, rugs or, in the case of older

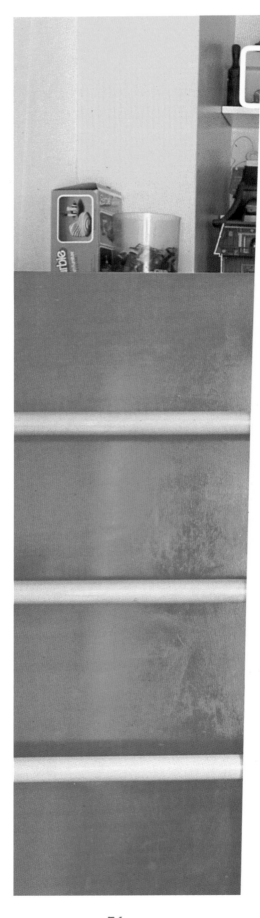

Above: For recreation, coordination and muscle development all in one package, it's hard to beat a prefabricated indoor jungle gym.

Left: A brightly painted staircase leads to a spacious overhead play world. This room plan, with its well-defined functional areas, encourages a fun-loving child to be tidy and self-sufficient.

children, a hammock.

Additional play areas can be developed as new inclinations develop. If, for example, your child takes up a musical instrument, you may want to add a three-sided, acoustically insulated practice nook to the room by placing a bookcase or something similar as a room divider near one corner at a right angle to the wall and covering the divider, the corner walls and the ceiling with thick cork tiles.

This type of functional play-room arrangement has several major advantages. It inspires children to make constructive choices about how to use their playtime. In providing well-defined territories, you allow several children occupying the room at the same time to pursue separate interests. It motivates children to keep their playroom neat and well-organized by making it clear where an item ultimately belongs, even if it is dragged out into the center of the room for an individual play session. Fi-nally, it serves as an ideal set-up for creating imaginative and practical wall and floor treatments.

In a playroom, you can afford to be more adventurous in decorating the walls than you can in a bedroom, where the decoration must not interfere with such quiet activities as sleeping or studying. Try highlighting each functional area with a different color of paint, a distinctive super-graphic or a representative wall hanging. Group full-

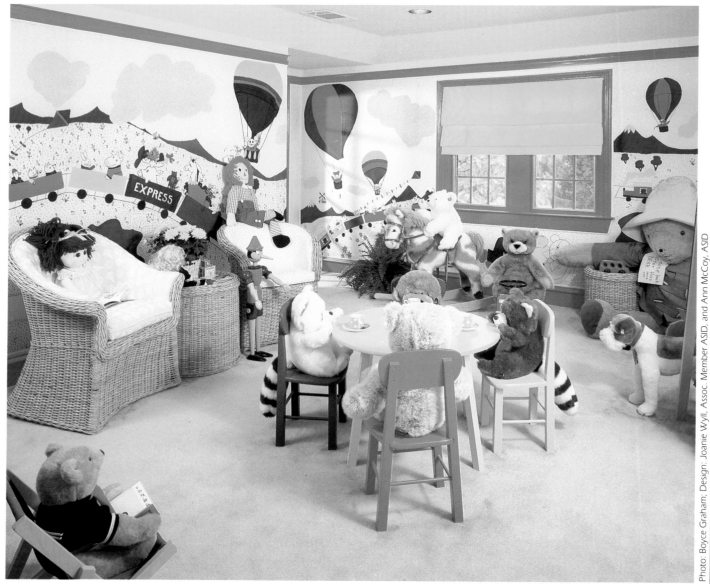

Photo: Boyce Graham; Design: Joanie Wyll, Assoc. Member ASID, and Ann McCoy, ASID

Facing page: This exuberant play-room owes much of its appeal to a teasing reversal of normal, adult-room decorating principles. The wooden trim and ceiling stand out in red and yellow, while the floor is covered with white carpeting and the walls are painted with a vibrant and delightfully captivating mural. The furnishings and play friends come in all shapes, sizes and colors, complementing this active decor no matter where they are situated.

Above: A recessed nook becomes a garage for play vehicles and an ir-regularly shaped wall supports lots of shelves for toy storage. The two areas are tied together by a spring-green wall treatment that looks es-pecially crisp and compelling set against white.

Facing page: A long, wide counter offers plenty of elbow room and play space for games, train tracks and other toys and was easy to build into the sloping wall of this rustic, all-wood kid's room. The overhead lights provide necessary task-directed illumination while the bulletin board reduces countertop paper clutter. *Below:* High-gloss enamel paint on the walls, mirror tiles on the ceiling and energetic supergraphics make this entire room a one-of-a-kind play space for a child with an active imagination.

Courtesy of Riviera Blinds

J. Michael Kanouff

At night, this wooden box-frame makes a handsome custom-sized junior bed for a young girl and her fuzzy stuffed friend.

length mirrors behind an exercise area. As a backdrop to a hobby- or workbench, fashion a three-dimensional mural that incorporates permanent wooden and plastic cutouts with places to hang tools.

Floors, too, can help to define and enliven different functional areas of the playroom. If the floor of the room consists of plain wooden planks, you can paint it with borders or patterns (such as a checkerboard or a hopscotch game) that fit specific areas. You can

also lay separate, compatible patterns of tile or linoleum in each area. Although it's a good idea to leave the center of the floor free of carpeting, you may want to position nonskid rugs or tack carpet sections in appropriate side spots, such as in a rest area.

Multilevel platforms are delightful features that fully enhance the spirit of a playroom. For a young child, platforms offer excellent and safe climbing practice. For children of every age, they furnish a wel-

come variety of activity stations. Build a series of platforms out of plywood and 2-by-4-inch wooden braces and glue indoor/outdoor carpeting to all surfaces. These platforms can then be stacked in one corner or used to line the perimeter of the room. To prevent nasty spills, be sure that each platform level is not wide enough or long enough for a child to run on. A different color of carpeting for each platform level will make the drop-off points clearly visible.

During the day, the same wooden box turned on one side becomes a giant chalkboard to share with a real-life friend.

J. Michael Kanouff

John Driemen

With the bunk beds tucked into the narrow end of the room, this ingenious design allows two sisters maximum play space. The louvered doors enclose a substantial storage area.

Furniture for the playroom needs to be lightweight, sturdy and uncomplicated. Plastic tables, chairs and storage units can withstand a lot of hard use and are easy to move and clean. They're also inexpensive to replace as they become worn or as your children outgrow them.

You may want to include one item of furniture that is extraordinary and that gives the playroom a center of inter-est or a prevailing theme. This can be a merry-go-round pony, a large dollhouse, a car-nival booth that doubles as a playhouse and a puppet stage or a cleverly designed piece of exercise equipment.

If you don't have a separate playroom in your house, de-fine a specific play area in your child's bedroom with an ap-propriate decorative motif or a distinctive furnishing. For prac-tical reasons, the best location is a brightly lighted area as far away from the bed as possi-ble. The object of this strategy is not necessarily to confine play to only one section of your child's room. Instead, it is to inspire play by giving it special attention in the ar-rangement of the room, as well as to identify a space for storing play items. Children will play anywhere. Nevertheless, they will naturally gravitate toward a spot that is playful in itself.

Facing page: Two-dimensional al-phabet blocks on the walls and those of three dimensions on the table delight the eye and challenge the mind in this theme-oriented play space.

Above: A play space can be in-corporated into any room of the house. Here an ingeniously designed cabinet in a kitchen corner can be disassembled to form chair, table and storage units for children.

A Portable Playhouse

Young children love having a room-within-a-room. It's a special space that can be anything they want it to be: a home of their own, a fort, a store, a school, a hospital or an office. This playhouse has three sides and is designed to stand against a wall. Because it folds flat, it's easy to store and move. You can even set it up outdoors next to a side of the house.

1. Cut a 5-by-6-foot sheet of ¾-inch plywood. This will become the front of the playhouse.

2. Cut two sheets of ¾-inch plywood that are 5-by-2¾ feet each. These will become the sides of the playhouse.

3. Cut one strip of ½-inch plywood that is 1½ inches wide and 5 feet long.

4. Cut a 4-by-1½-foot doorway out of the 5-by-6-foot sheet of plywood, so that the right edge of the doorway forms a perpendicular line midway along the 6-foot side. Make sure the cut is a clean one so that you can use the cut piece itself for the door.

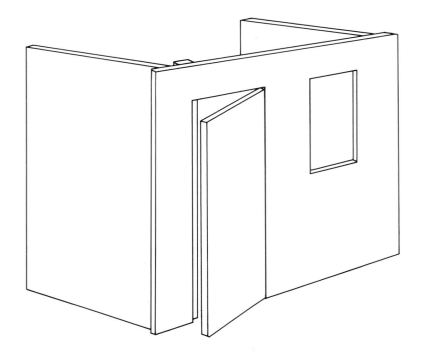

5. Cut a 1-by-1½-foot window into the center of the other end of the 5-by-6-foot plywood sheet, so that the top of the window is even with the top of the door.

6. Attach each of the side panels to one end of the front of the playhouse with 2 hinges.

7. Position the 1½-inch-by-5-foot strip of plywood on the back side of the 5-by-6-foot sheet of plywood so that it runs along the right edge of the doorway with half of its width extending into the door space. Nail it securely into place. This will provide both a prop for the door itself and stability for the front of the playhouse as a whole.

8. Attach the door to the front of the playhouse with hinges on the left side of the door frame, so that it swings outward. Attach a door handle.

9. Paint all surfaces with a durable paint. You may want to paint the inside and outside with different colors, but avoid painting any details that will establish the playhouse as a particular type of building. This will enable your child to imagine whatever he or she wishes.

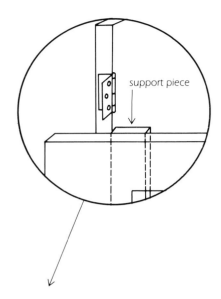

support piece

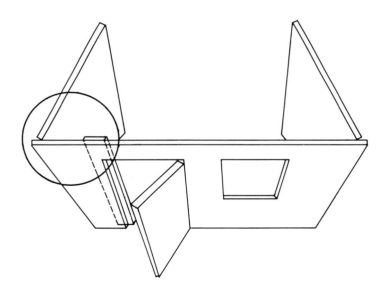

Photo: Phillip Ennis. Design: Ronald Bricke & Associates, Inc.

CHAPTER 5
Study Areas

hen children begin their formal education, they learn to distinguish between work (reading, writing and arithmetic) and play (recess, gym and free time). It is an inevitable step toward becoming an adult.

At home, school-age kids respond to this discovery by wanting a space in their bedroom deliberately set aside for study, similar to the kind they have in their classroom. They especially appreciate a well-designed study area that makes this challenging transition period between child-

hood and adulthood as pleasant as possible. For younger children, a study area is a comfortable, private environment in which they can develop good study habits by practicing the behaviors and activities of learning. For older children, it's a quiet, secluded spot to do homework, explore individual interests and conduct personal business.

The best location in the room for a study space is one that is well away from the door and from any play area that might create a distraction. Situating a desk in a corner or building it into an alcove saves

Venetian blinds hung from metal crossbeams divide this teenager's large basement bedroom into functional subsections, including a well-outfitted study area in back.

Photo: Mike Nicholson/EWA; Design: (tk)

Right: The visual uniformity created by a wall of bookshelves in this study area is relieved by cascading ferns, planted in boxes and lit by flourescent ceiling lights.

Left: Wicker furniture creates a separate, nontraditional area for reading and writing in this young girl's bedroom.

Above: **This desk is bordered on two sides by wall surfaces that can be used as bulletin boards, keeping the desk surface clear of unnecessary clutter.** *Facing page:* **Sleek, built-in desk space in front of a window is efficient, unobtrusive and a pleasure to work in.**

space. Stay away from dark, cramped spots where the user may not want to spend much time. A site near a window is ideal.

The basic furnishings of an effective study space are a desk (or table with drawers), bookshelves, a lamp, a wastebasket and a board to post notes—most commonly a cork-lined bulletin board. Depending on your child's preference, there are two ways to outfit the space: either by purchasing or building a desk complex or acquiring each component separately. The latter option allows greater freedom to move or change individual items. The former option offers a more well-defined and efficient use of available space.

A desk complex is a single freestanding unit that contains a table and drawers, bookshelves and, usually, a bulletin board—all carefully and compactly arranged so that there is plenty of room to spread out papers and books and keep everything easily accessible. Most forest product and furniture companies manufacture desk complexes, but many parents choose to build a desk complex themselves, with the input and help of their children. It's an excellent opportunity to create a unique and adaptable study area that fits beautifully into the child's bedroom.

If you choose to acquire each component separately, give special consideration to the desk. There are many different types available, including all-wood desks, all-metal

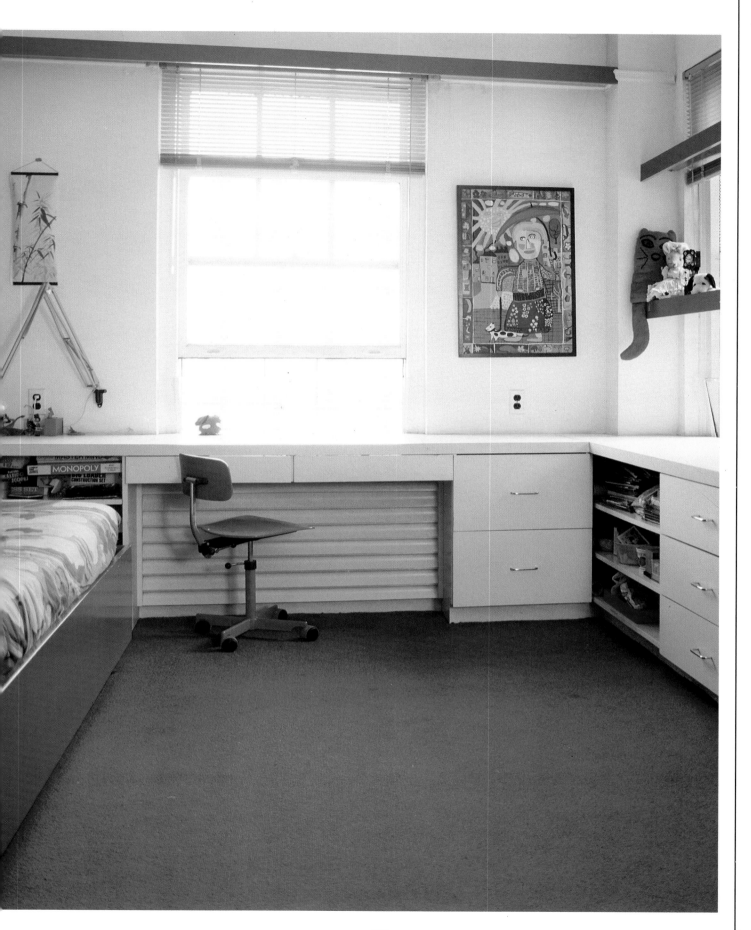

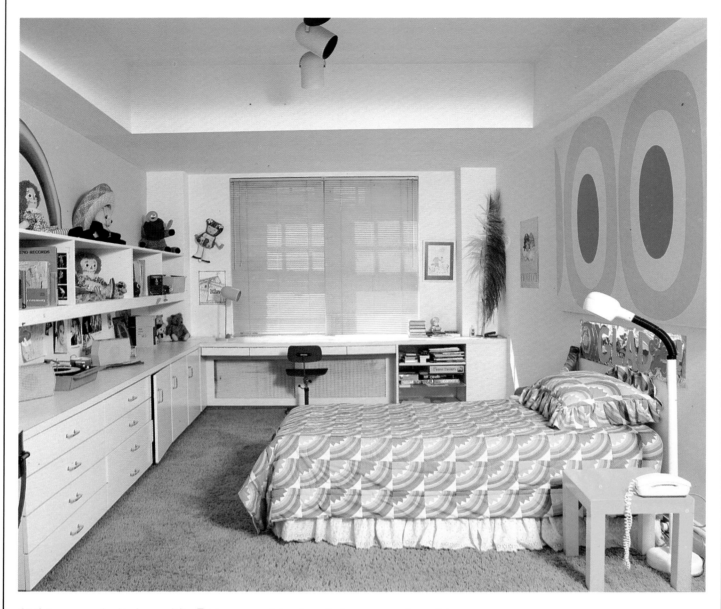

desks, wood desks with For-
mica tops, rolltop desks, desks
with one pedestal of drawers,
desks with two pedestals of
drawers (called "kneehole"
desks) and desks with adjustable tops (either adjustable in
height, in angle or both). You
may want to buy a commer-
cial desk in any one of hun-
dreds of different design styles,
or purchase a piece of school
furniture, or construct your
own desk, which may involve
simply fitting a wooden board
across the top of two chests or

cabinets of drawers. An older
child may need a desk that is
designed to hold a typewriter
or a computer, unless these
components are kept on separate tables. To help promote
the enjoyment of studying,
make certain that you choose
a desk your child really likes.

Chairs also come in a wide
variety of shapes, sizes and
styles. Select any straight-
backed chair that is comfortable and that harmonizes well
with the desk. Many children
are particularly fond of swivel

Above: A large, silk-screened canvas
wall hanging, coordinating color
blinds and a paper rainbow define
respectively the sleep, study and
play environments of this bedroom.

Facing page: Simple components fit
snugly together in this space-saving
study corner. Color highlights in a
basic all-white design help the area
appear uncluttered and attractive.

76

chairs, which help to relieve the feeling of being "pinned down" at the desk. Avoid high-intensity, track or goose-neck lamps in favor of one with a good-sized shade that can supply bright light over a broad surface. Bookshelves should be placed so that books are within plain sight and at arm's length of the desk chair. A bookcase to the side of the desk or adjustable, wall-mounted shelves above the desk will allow for just this sort of easy access.

If two children share a room, you might consider purchasing two desk carrels. Typically found in university libraries, a desk carrel consists of a desk with overhanging shelves that is encased in panels, giving it visual and acoustical privacy. An alternative is to construct separate study cubicles using bookshelves as space dividers.

A study desk should be reserved for studying and not for playing or working on a hobby. If possible, provide additional table space in the room for nonstudy use. It's also advisable to set up a comfortable chair next to a bright light for reading. If there is another room in the house that your child can have private use of, gradually shift recreational items to that room and make his or her bedroom increasingly associated with learning. The more the physical look and atmosphere of a specific place suggests quiet concentration, the more encouraged your child will be to study there.

Right: This young grade-schooler finds schoolwork less daunting with some of her play friends around to encourage her. *Below:* A miniature built-in office grouping, complete with a separate computer table, offers this student lots of support for pursuing any academic activity.

Paul Johnson

Below: Cindy's thru-port desk takes maximum advantage of a small corner and gives her fingertip access to all her study aides.

Photo: Bruce Glass; Design: [tk]

Building a Desk

A desk that is attractive in design and handmade by a parent is doubly appealing to the young student. This desk includes side and back guards and open shelves that help a child to keep things tidy and well-organized.

1. Cut two 36-by-20-inch pieces of 1-inch plywood. These pieces will be the two ends of the desk.

2. Cut a triangular section out of the top of each end piece, along a line extending 1 inch from one corner to a point 6 inches below the corner across from it.

3. Cut one 29-by-19-inch piece of 1-inch plywood. This will be the left panel of the shelving unit.

4. Cut one 55-by-19-inch piece of 1-inch plywood. This will be the top surface of the desk.

5. Cut one 55-by-15-inch piece of 1-inch plywood. This will be the back guard of the desk.

6. Cut three 16-by-19-inch pieces of 1-inch plywood. These will be the shelves.

7. Cut 2 triangular pieces of 1-inch plywood that are 6 inches long on each side of a right angle. These will be supports for the well of the desk.

8. Cut one 16-by-5-inch piece of 1-inch plywood. This will be a support for the top of the shelving unit.

9. Build the shelving unit by nailing the shelves between the left panel piece and the right end piece, using 2 evenly spaced 4-penny nails on each side of each shelf. Begin by nailing the bottom shelf 2 inches above the ground, so that the 16-inch side faces outward and is flush with the outside edges of the panel

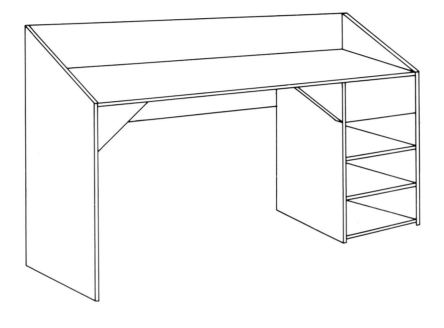

and the end piece. Nail the second shelf 6 inches above the bottom shelf and the third shelf 6 inches above the second shelf.

10. Nail the support for the top of the shelving unit between the left panel and the right end piece, facing outward, so that the surface of the support is flush with the edges of the panel and the end piece. The top corners of the support should be flush with the top of the left panel and the top of the right end piece.

11. Nail the desk top to the right end piece and the left shelving unit panel, using 3 evenly spaced 4-penny nails for each attachment. The outward edge of the desk top should be flush with the outward edge of the end piece and panel.

12. Nail the left end piece to the desk top with 3 evenly spaced 4-penny nails.

13. Nail the back guard in place between the 2 end pieces with 4-penny nails: 3 vertically at each end piece, 2 vertically at the shelving unit panel, and horizontally along the desk top every 5 inches. The top of the back guard should be flush with the top of each end piece, so that the triangle at each end piece begins descending where the 2 surfaces meet.

14. Nail the triangular well supports into place between the desk top and the sides of the desk well, so that the surface of each triangle is flush with the edge of the desk top and the edge of the end piece or shelving panel to which it is attached.

15. Paint the desk with a brightly colored, chip-resistant enamel paint.

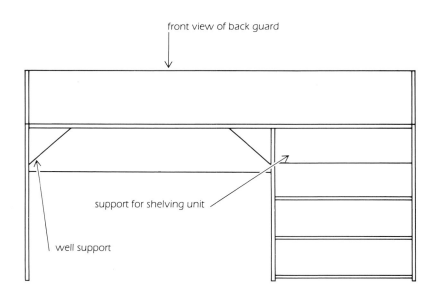

front view of back guard

support for shelving unit

well support

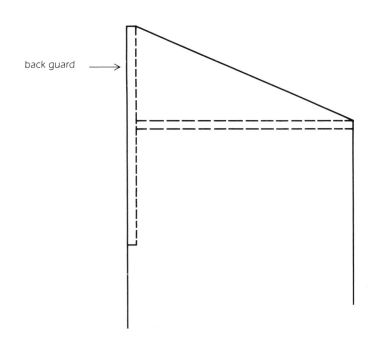

side view of back guard

back guard

Courtesy of Levolor Lorentzen/Wall Tex

CHAPTER 6
Storage Spaces

I n the popular imagination, a kid's room always looks as if it's just been struck by a tornado. The parent repeatedly squawks at the child to clean it up. The child repeatedly expends the least amount of effort to achieve the minimum standard of order. The door to the room is always kept closed when company visits.

Even if a child is tidy by nature, the sheer variety of colors, patterns, textures, sizes and shapes among the contents likely to be found in his or her room can dizzy the senses. Kids accumulate hordes of toys, clothes and plain old stuff. No matter how carefully each item is arranged, the total mass may still give the impression of clutter.

Whichever of these two descriptions fits your child's room, an abundance of attractive and carefully planned storage spaces is a major asset. It not only adds to the overall effectiveness of the room (by increasing, for instance, the available floor space), but also motivates your child to keep the room neat and orderly on a continual basis.

A cardinal rule in creating good storage spaces is never to forget that these areas are activity centers. Kids are constantly moving to and from storage spaces. While they are there they bend, stretch, grope, grab, stack, sort, open and close. Be sure each storage area is easily accessible in relation to the flow of traffic in the room, and simple yet sturdy in construction. A box

Left: Vinyl-sheathed metal closet organizers make versatile and attractive storage units both inside and outside the closet.

Right: Wooden shelves have been built into this closet, giving the user a customized vanity table in addition to strong, distinctive storage cabinets.

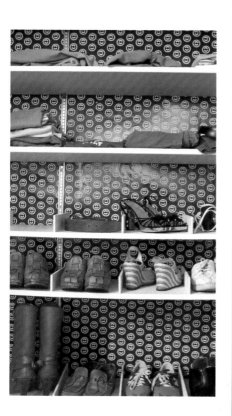

Right: Here, bracketed shelves have been subdivided for stashing small items quickly and easily. Patterned contact paper makes a lively backdrop.

Positioning a cutaway dollhouse on top of a similarly proportioned shelving unit gives the unit a more playful look, as well as motivates the user to make a game out of cleaning up.

with a flat lid on top that can be wheeled across the floor may be much better for storing toys than a heavy, stationary cupboard with a multipart latch. It may make much more sense to put a chest of drawers for clothes right next to the clothes closet than at the opposite end of the room.

A storage space is also a display area. Items that are visually appealing or stimulating deserve to remain in plain view. The ever-present sight of decorative blocks on an eye-level shelf, for example, will inspire dozens of fantasy buildings in the mind of a young child. More utilitarian items need to be well organized within their storage spaces so that each specific article can be located at a glance. Numerous small containers and cubbyholes may offer more satisfactory display for school supplies and clothes than a few large, open drawers, where everything can get dumped in a heap.

Most storage schemes rely on a balanced combination of shelves, cupboards (meaning any small enclosed space, such as a chest, bureau or box), closets and racks (including pegboards, bulletin boards and hang posts). The more options you present, the more inviting it will be for your child to devise and execute his or her own personal storage strategies.

Young kids in particular appreciate low, open shelves where much-used items can be placed within easy reach. A wall-mounted shelf system of metal standards with detachable brackets is especially practical because it can be readjusted as the child grows bigger. Above the shelves, you can set up cabinets with doors for storing play materials that require adult assistance, like paints, scissors and paste.

Wooden cupboards, consisting of flat panels nailed to simple beam frames, can be custom-built to fit an otherwise useless corner or a narrow space between two doors. Modular vinyl cupboard units come in a wide

Plastic containers in a variety of sizes and colors keep individual playthings neatly grouped together and are convenient for kids to carry to and from play areas.

Photo: Durston Saylor; Design: Joan Halprin

range of sizes, shapes and styles. Aside from being colorful, lightweight and virtually indestructible, they are easy to maintain and can be assembled in many configurations to suit a child's changing moods and needs.

Vinyl- or rubber-coated wire frame baskets and racks, known collectively as "closet organizers," provide excellent storage alternatives for kids' rooms, both inside and outside the closet. If your child's room has a large walk-in closet, you can put a chest of drawers against the back wall and create a private, space-saving dressing nook. A clothes tree looks nice and offers a resting place for sports equipment, toys and tools, as well as clothes. Children of all ages enjoy hanging things on pegs, whether the pegs are

supported by a shaft or a railing, nailed directly into wall studs or slotted into a pegboard.

A child requires so much personal storage space that it can tend to overpower other, more interesting features of the room. The solution is to search for ingenious ways to conceal or camouflage individual storage areas. Buy or build furniture that has storage space incorporated into the design: for example, a chair with a cupboard beneath the

seat or a table with a hinged top that lifts to reveal a large single drawer. Paint a toy chest to resemble a cage of tigers. Paper a bureau with the same paper that covers the wall behind it. Skillfully managed, storing things can become a now-you-see-it-now-you-don't game at which your child will be enthusiastic.

Facing page, far left: This wall space, above trimly lined storage cabinets, is a perfect place to mount a bicycle and an excellent example of unconventional but highly efficient use of space.

Courtesy of Motif Designs

Above: Duffel bags are a handy and neat means of storing stuff beneath a bed. Here a set of bags, which restates the wallpaper design in different colors, is as attractive as it is practical.

Right: Sports equipment seems right at home in these commercial storage lockers. Individual units can be rearranged to suit a number of different storage-space set-ups.

Courtesy of Charmglow

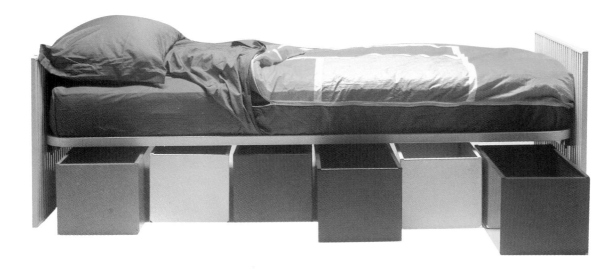

Above: Cubic storage boxes slide under a bed easily and make excellent use of normally forgotten or poorly utilized storage space.

Left: Here bracket shelves are recessed into a column that frames one side of a mirrored dressing table; the shelves enhance the dimensions of the table and remove clutter from its surface.

Facing page: Ample space below an elevated bed is meticulously designed for maximum storage utility in this narrow wing of a child's room. Each shelf has been faced with a strip that picks up the finish on the wooden ladder and bed railing.

An imaginative color scheme offsets
the massive bulk of this storage
wall, giving it the appearance of a
Mondrian sculpture. The artful design is repeated in the adjacent
poster.

Clutter

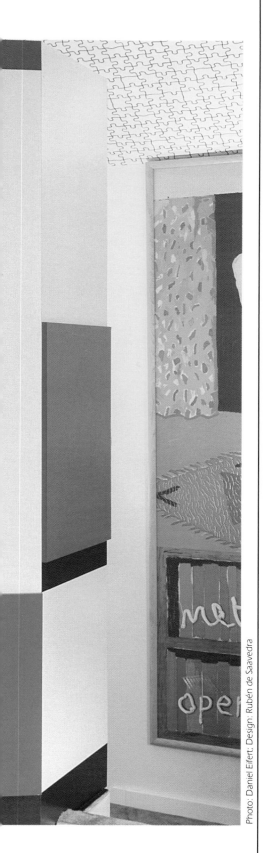

• Construct 3 shallow, lidless boxes approximately 1½-by-2-feet long out of ¾-inch plywood, or purchase wooden or plastic boxes of equivalent dimensions. Use them to store toys, play materials, clothes or shoes under the bed. Use similar boxes to fit beneath bureaus, bookcases and other bulky pieces of furniture.

• Collect baskets of various shapes, sizes and styles and group them in different "activity zones" around the room. One group of baskets, for example, can be placed near a desk to hold books, papers and writing implements. Another group can be situated in a play area to hold dolls, games and toys. A third group can be set up next to a closet to hold different kinds of play clothes, wraps or costumes.

• Buy a large folding screen with an imaginative design, or build one out of plywood sheets or heavy fabric stretched over a plywood frame. Use the screen to mark off and conceal a storage area in a corner of the room.

• Buy a tall metal school locker. Paint it with a single bright color and use it to stash sports equipment, coats or hobby materials.

• Create a "storage wall." Take a large pegboard and draw colorful, actual-size outlines of different items, such as tools, across the board. Each outline should indicate where that particular item should hang, either on hooks stuck into the holes of the pegboard or through loops tied through the holes. Then mount the board on the wall so that it can be easily reached by your child. The board will look even more attractive, particularly when it's fairly empty, if you attach boldly painted wooden symbols (such as stars, shields or hearts) here and there among the tool mounts.

• Suspend a hammock or piece of strong netting shaped like a hammock from sturdy hooks screwed deeply into wall supports. It can run either between walls that are directly opposite each other or between adjacent walls. Use the hammock to store dolls, stuffed animals, play equipment, toys and clothing that are not likely to get easily entangled in the mesh.

• Construct a bike rack on the wall with metal angle irons. Screw 2 of them deep into wall studs just far enough apart to support the bike securely (a distance that varies according to the bike's design and where it's best for the irons to go). Place the irons high enough on the wall so that the bike is out of the way but still convenient to take down. If you feel it's safe, you can provide a stool or small stepladder for this purpose.

CHAPTER 7
Furniture

At some point early in the process of planning your child's room, it's a good idea to get down on your knees and shuffle around the other rooms of your house. This gives you some appreciation of how standard-size furniture looks from a kid's point of view. Children spend a hefty percentage of their time in a world that overwhelms them, reinforcing their feelings of powerlessness and alienation.

Parents can help compensate for this experience by outfitting their children's rooms with furniture that is designed for kids. This means replacing individual items every few years as your child develops physically and mentally. It also means buying or building furniture that is adjustable, such as tables with several sets of legs in different lengths.

At all times you need to consider the special relationships that children have with furniture. Since children enjoy a variety of tactile experiences, give your child "soft" furniture—such as a futon or a bean-bag chair—as well as "hard" furniture. Make sure that wooden chairs are sturdy enough to stand on. Paint the undersides of all furniture, so that they're attractive when viewed from floor-level. Favor lightweight pieces and equip heavier pieces with ball-bearing castors or glides so that your child can easily re-arrange the floor plan. Mount lamps, shelves and even tables on the walls so that your child has more room to roam around in.

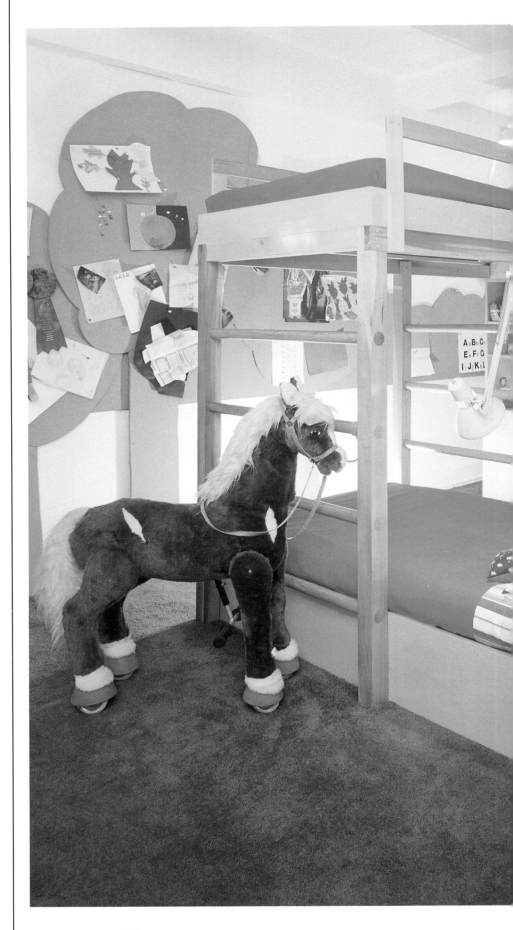

Above: Furniture that has a lot of visual and tactile appeal—like this unique bureau-and-shelf unit of wood, wicker and brass—is ideal for a young child who is just beginning to explore the boundaries of his or her domain.

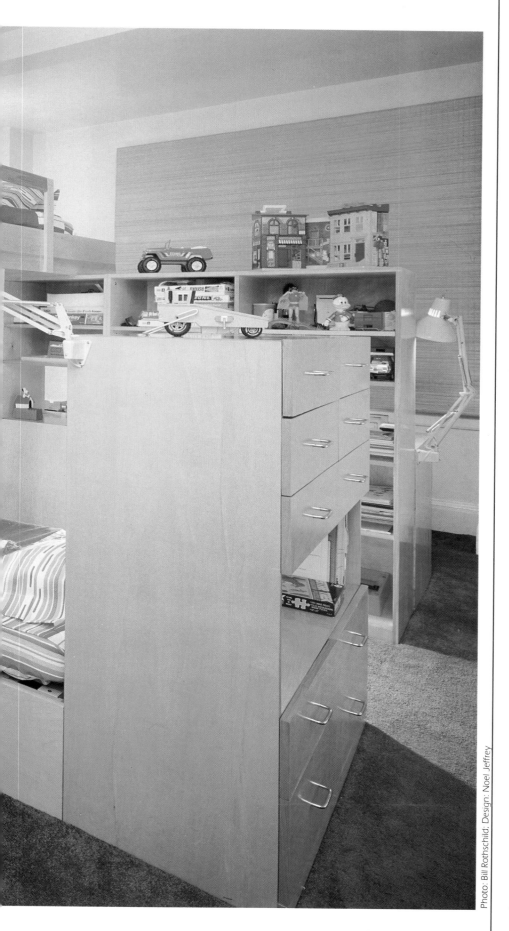

Left: A freestanding complex containing two beds, two sets of drawers, two desks and plenty of shelves provides ample floor space and personal privacy in this room for two boys. Note the use of corkboard cutouts and industrial carpeting to protect the walls and floors and make them more serviceable.

John Driemen

Above: Easy-to-construct wooden steps and platforms create a wonderfully different environment for playing, lounging, sleeping and storing important toys. This kind of arrangement is especially effective in a large, plain room that lacks any architectural distinction. *Facing page, top:* Concealed storage units in the wall and in a small, carpet-covered storage platform keep the play space tidy. *Facing page, bottom:* A toy chest also can be a safe and delightful hiding place.

A child's taste in furniture style is notoriously fickle. Specific items of furniture are apt to be replaced or altered at unpredictable intervals, not only because the child outgrows them but also because they're subject to a great deal of rough use. For these reasons it's best to avoid antiques, costly designer furniture and matched suites of furnishings. Above all, choose individual pieces that are relatively simple and clean in design. They will wear better than more elaborate pieces and are more likely to stay compatible with their surroundings over the years. For the sake of aesthetics, remember to vary the overall shapes of these pieces. A room full of nothing but rectangular, circular, horizontal or vertical furniture is deadening to the senses.

If you and your child have your hearts set on something more grandiose, you can satisfy that desire and remain practical by being very selective. One especially dramatic piece of furniture—a brightly colored throne with intricately carved dragon legs, for example—is enough to lend a kid's room a distinctive touch of fantasy or elegance. To intensify the effect, you can echo some of the colors or designs of the focal piece elsewhere in the room, such as in the wall treatment or in trim that you apply to a bookcase or a bedstead.

The most important point in choosing or building any piece of furniture for a child's room is safety—for the child

John Driemen

John Driemen

Photo: Karen Bussolini; Painting & Stenciling: John Canning

Photo: Karen Bussolini; Painting & Stenciling: John Canning

Photo: Karen Bussolini; Painting: John Canning

Above left: This simple, uncluttered kid's room is personalized by hand-painted details on the wooden floor and chest of drawers. *Top right:* The side of the chest is appropriately painted with a bucolic scene that greets whoever enters the room and melds wonderfully with the wooden door and flooring.

Bottom right: Each drawer of the chest offers a different scene, creating an inventive and playful piece of furniture.

Heavy oak and walnut pieces lend warmth and security to this kid's room. They also harmonize well with the handsome wooden floor, wall trim and ceiling beams.

Photo: Bill Rothschild; Design: Noel Jeffrey

Photo: Courtesy of Dragons of Walton Street

Top: Child-sized plastic furniture groupings are sturdy, safe, easy-to-clean and economical.

Bottom: This attractive table-and-chairs set has been lovingly painted to charm the young host.

and for the piece of furniture itself. Stay clear of furniture with sharp corners or thin, breakable limbs or projections. Joints in bureaus, chairs and tables should be dovetailed or locked, rather than glued. All legs should be held in place with corner blocks. Large items should sit firmly on the floor and not rock or tip easily.

The finish on a piece of child's furniture needs to be chip- and crack-resistant, as well as easy to clean. Plastic laminates (such as acrylic paints) are ideal and simple to apply yourself. When purchasing vinyl-covered chairs or plastic tables and chairs, check to be certain that the plastic is bound to a backing for stability.

Furniture in a child's room is not like furniture anywhere else. When your child is very young, you have to expect that the furniture will be damaged. When your child is a teenager, you have to allow for the possibility that some of the furniture will be taken away to his or her first independent living quarters. As long as you don't assume that a piece of children's furniture is there to stay, and stick to items that are simple, sturdy and safe, you'll be doing fine.

This eye-catching color-spectrum table is both practical and decorative, and fits perfectly into a room full of playful geometric shapes.

Each piece of furniture here—the junior bed frame, the chest of drawers and the side table—has been carefully designed to occupy its particular space. Strong, clean lines and a bold use of primary colors give the ensemble a style and energy that will stay fresh for years.

Courtesy of Levolor Lorentzen

Above: This arrangement of modular couches, hassocks and tables at one end of the bedroom is a versatile sitting and playing area during the day and a place for overnight guests to sleep at night.

Right: This fine oak headboard functions as a centerpiece for the bedroom, defining the sleeping space and investing it with warmth and solidity.

Building A Clothes Rack

Children love furniture that you've made for them, especially furniture that's unique to a child's world. This clothes rack stands securely by itself anywhere in the room and is perfect for a youngster who needs an incentive to develop good organizational habits. It's attractive in its own right and will be a welcome addition to any room.

1. Cut two 55-inch lengths of ¾-by-8-inch pine. These will be the sides of the rack.

2. Cut a 40-inch length of ¾-by-8-inch pine. This will be the top shelf of the rack.

3. Cut a 38½-inch length of ¾-by-8-inch pine. This will be the bottom shelf of the rack.

4. Cut a 38½-inch length of ¾-by-4-inch pine. This will be the support below the bottom shelf.

5. Using a band saw (or comparable hand tool), cut the 6 ornamental side pieces (2 of each design), 4 triangular supports and 2 bases according to the grid shown below and on the top of page 107.

6. Using wood glue, attach the ornamental side pieces to the outer surface of the 2 sides of the rack. Space the 3 pieces evenly on each side.

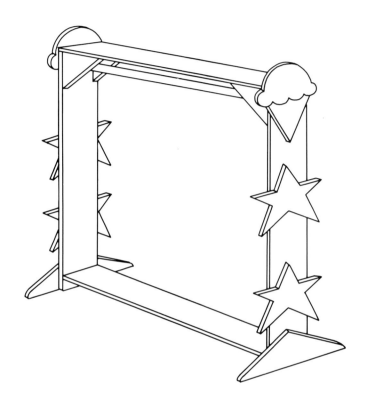

grid for ornamental side pieces

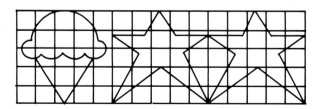

grid for bases

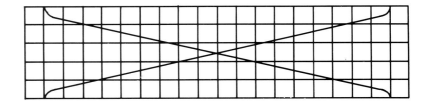

7. Nail the top shelf of the rack to the sides with 3 evenly spaced 6-penny nails on each side.

8. Nail the support for the bottom shelf to each of the sides. It should be nailed directly in the center of each side, flush with the bottom of the side, so that the support stands 4 inches vertically.

9. Nail the bottom shelf to each of the sides so that it rests firmly on the support. Use 3 evenly spaced 6-penny nails. Then nail the bottom shelf to the support, using 5 evenly spaced 6-penny nails.

grid for triangular supports

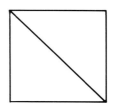

10. Install a 38½-inch closet pole with closet pole brackets and screws about 4 inches below the top shelf in the center of each side. Then nail the triangular supports in place, just inside the top corners of each side (front and back of the rack).

11. Nail the base securely to the bottom of each side, using 3 evenly spaced nails.

12. Paint the entire rack with durable acrylic paint, using different colors for the 2 shelves and the ornamental side pieces.

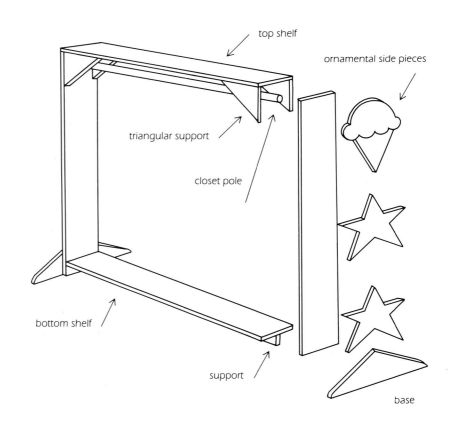

Photo: Phillip Ennis; Design: Ronald Bricke & Associates, Inc.

CHAPTER 8
Final Touches

To little people, little things definitely mean a lot. It's kinder on your budget and your child's imagination if you work to achieve most of the decorative effects in your child's room through small accessory details rather than through the main furnishings themselves. This is where a do-it-yourself talent comes in handy. Use fabric paints to create a striking lampshade design. Construct a wooden radiator shield that has rainbow-colored slats. Fashion a series of cushions featuring different textures: slippery satin, smooth leather, rugged corduroy, nubby tweed, soft fur, grainy denim, feathery velvet.

Quilts and comforters make wonderfully practical and appealing bedcovers. An especially vivid or intricate design can liven up the entire room. The same holds true for a patterned wall hanging, which can be anything from a sheet to a rug to a soft sculpture of macrame. Best of all, you can change bedcovers and wall hangings easily, periodically giving your child's room a whole new look.

Small objects that delight both the mind and the senses are particularly appropriate ornaments for a child's room. Put a prism or a piece of stained glass in front of a sunny window. Hang a mobile on the ceiling above a play table. Place an old-fashioned cash register or set of scales on a stand of its own. Attach a barometer or clock to the wall.

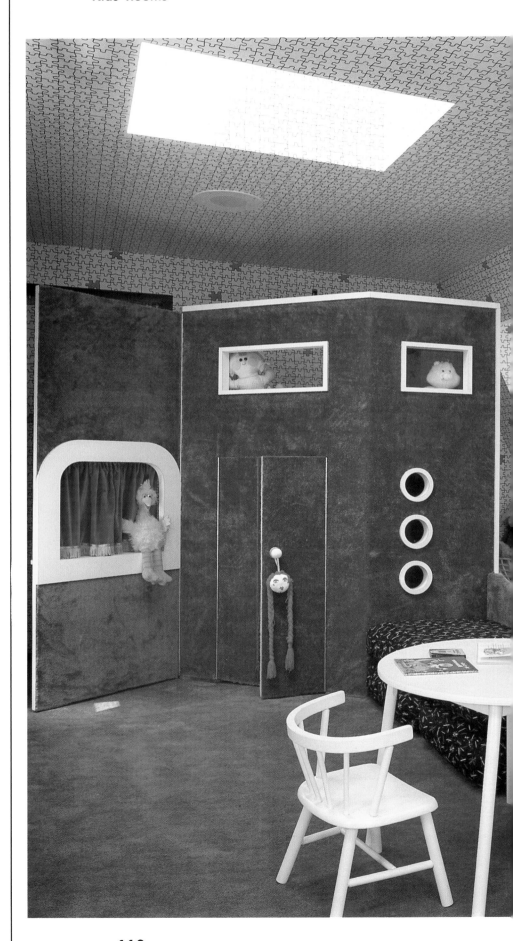

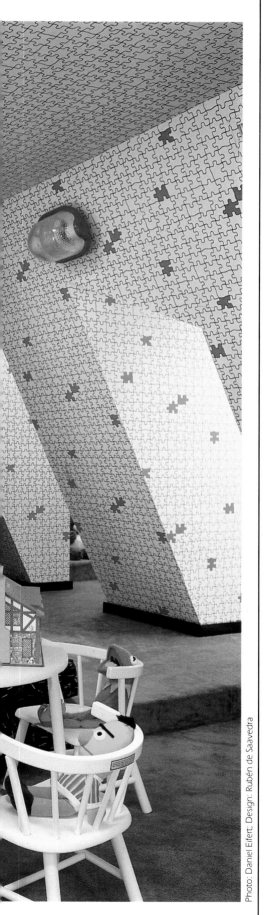

Left: This portable, freestanding playhouse is the defining element in this oddly shaped room, demarcating play space and creating much-welcomed nooks and cranies to explore and utilize. *Above:* This room is packed with details that are fun and instructive—including a super-graphic with the orderly colors of the rainbow, an aquarium and a balsa model of a Tyrannosaurus rex.

Above: A large wooden rooster is a bookend, a pencil holder and a toy all rolled into one.

Right: The top of a peg rack supports painted wooden cutouts, which you can buy or make yourself with the aid of a jigsaw.

An ornamental shelf allows a child to spotlight his or her favorite possessions. This wrought-iron example is sizable without being bulky.

Facing page: **This ingenious storage mechanism for toys is constructed from a metal framework and heavy rope.**

Above: **A wall of hats and helmets for make-believe games is a pleasure to look at. Note that the surface around each peg is outlined so the appropriate hat can be returned to the right place.**

Right: **A pole of hooks for storing stuffed animals saves space and offers a satisfying display of this child's complete menagerie. A ring has been attached to each animal for easy hanging.**

Small furnishings that are pretty as well as functional—a child-size easel or a stepping stool—are also excellent room accents. Young children can play with simple boxes and boards for hours. Brightly colored and well-finished, these objects have an abstract sculptural quality that can be very handsome, no matter how they are left to lie around.

Dollhouses and puppet stages do triple duty in virtually any child's room: They provide entertainment, education and beauty. Even better, you and your child can enjoy them together on an ongoing basis, purchasing or making either tiny pieces of furniture for the dollhouse or puppet clothes and props for the puppet stage.

Exercising your own ingenuity in creating a pleasant room for your child is important. Your child will treasure any token of your handicraft. What gives a kid's room its unique charm and character, however, is the personal contribution the child makes to its decor. Children are natural creators and collectors, and they instinctively want to leave their own stamp on their living space. They may sketch pictures they like to see on their walls. They may amass a horde of unusual rocks they love to touch. They may have a huge second family of stuffed animals they enjoy visiting with. You can take advantage of these interests by buying or building shelves, racks or frames that properly show off these artworks and collections.

Below: Posters, wall hangings and ribbons strung across a ceiling beam help define the activity areas in this compact but well-organized room.

Paul Johnson

An unusual pastel-colored wallcovering is the basis of the color scheme in this pleasingly functional child's room. The pattern is repeated in the curtains and the colors are picked up in the comforter and pillows. The light-colored wood of the wall unit also integrates well with the design.

Nothing has as much impact on the atmosphere of a room as lighting. In a kid's room especially—so full of different colors, shapes and textures—small lighting devices can make a world of difference. Install photocell night-lights in floor-level outlets. Use an electricity-operated lantern to illuminate a play space. Light up a dark corner with a globe of the constellations that glows in the dark.

The challenge in putting final touches to a child's room is to provide interesting details without creating clutter. Restrict yourself to a few items that will have impact. Take toys, furnishings and accessories that are no longer or rarely used out of the room and replace them with small decorative items that will give the room a fresh face. A child's life is full of changes, and his or her room should reflect this in a positive, imaginative and magical manner.

Facing page: **Small items require special showcases, like this printer's drawer hung from a wall.**

Top right: **Odd nooks and corners can be transformed into magical places. Here a long, low, built-in set of shelves turns otherwise dead space into a natural home for small stuffed creatures.**

Right: **Even the smallest changes make your child feel his or her world is special. This is doubly true in the case of intriguing, multipart mechanical equipment, like a telephone.**

Photo: Karen Bussolini; Painting: John Canning

Displaying Collections

• Buy or build frames with nonreflective glass covers to display special drawings or paintings or the best items in a stamp, coin, baseball card or photo collection. Place them in clusters in easily visible locations on the walls. It looks very attractive to have a shelf or table surface directly below wall-mounted frames where you can place freestanding frames with additional collection items.

• Buy or build shallow cases with glass covers on hinges and mount them on the wall. Use them to house collections of small objects, such as stones, ceramics or shells.

• To show off a collection of model cars, exotic dolls or unusual handicrafts, buy or build small, triangular shelves that fit snugly into a corner.

• Make your own stands and platforms. Build frames out of two-by-fours; nail plywood sheets to the frames, and then cover with carpeting. Use them to create multileveled display surfaces for dolls, sculptures and other relatively large collectibles. You may want to offer special focused-beam lighting for the area as a whole.

• Hang a large single-colored sheet, blanket or banner from the ceiling or the wall. Use it to display a button collection.

• Paint a stepladder with an elegant design and use it to support a collection of dolls, puppets or stuffed animals.

• Build or buy a room divider that has see-through cubbyholes. Place collectibles that are fairly large and can be viewed with interest from either side of the divider (such as driftwood, rocks, models or sculptures) in the open spaces. If appropriate, you may want to use the room divider to set apart a particular nook where the child can work on his or her collection.

• Put special paintings, photos, sheets of stamps and other flat collectibles under a transparent acrylic sheet that rests securely on a table top, forming a sturdy, easily cleaned table surface.

• Build a single thin shelf across the upper part of a window to display a collection of glass objects. The effect of sunlight streaming through each item is even more pleasing if the shelf itself is transparent (made either of glass or plastic).

Courtesy of United Wallcoverings

Above: **Here planters are put to an unusual use, complementing the airborne theme in the wallpaper.**

Facing page: **A single wall-mounted shelf becomes a perch for this fanciful doll arrangement—a scene that dresses up one whole side of the room.**

Sources
and Index

**Advance Furniture
Manufacturing Company**
24180 South Vermont Ave.
Harbour City, CA 90710
furniture

American of Martinsville
P.O. Box 5071
Martinsville, VA 24112
furniture

**American Plywood
Association**
1119 A Street
Tacoma, WA 98401
trade association

**American Toy and
Furniture Company, Inc.**
5933-T North Lincoln Avenue
Chicago, IL 60659
furniture, play equipment

Bright Industries
1900 NW First
P.O. Box 758
Boca Raton, FL 33432
wood products

Century Family Products
3628 Crenshaw Boulevard
Los Angeles, CA 90016
furniture, wood products

Childcraft Center
150 East 58th Street
New York, NY 10022
furniture, play equipment

**Child Life Play
Specialties, Inc.**
55 Whitney Street
Holliston, MA 01746
furniture, play equipment

The Children's Room, Inc.
318 East 45th Street
New York, NY 10017
furniture, play equipment

The Children's Workbench
470 Park Avenue South
New York, NY 10016
furniture, play equipment

Clairson International
5100 West Kennedy Blvd.
Tampa, FL 33609
wood products

Community Playthings
Route 213
Rifton, NY 12471
play equipment

**Albert Constantine
and Son, Inc.**
2050 Eastchester Road
Bronx, NY 10461
furniture

Constructive Playthings
1040 East 85th Street
Kansas City, MO 64131
play equipment

**Craftsman Wood Service
Company**
2727 South Mary Street
Chicago, IL 60608
wood products

Creative Playthings
1 East 53rd Street
New York, NY 10022
play equipment

Design Research
53 East 57th Street
New York, NY 10022
furniture

East-West Design, Inc.
Box 6022
Madison, WI 53716
furniture

Englander Company
558 Vandalia
St. Paul, MN 55114
furniture

**A.T. Euster Furniture
Company**
3300 NE Second Avenue
Miami, FL 33137
furniture

Fact and Fantasy Ltd.
325 Clemantis Street
West Palm Beach, FL 33401
furniture

Ficks Reed Company
4900 Charlemar Drive
Cincinnati, OH 45227
furniture

Forms and Surfaces, Inc.
P.O. Box 5215
Santa Barbara, CA 93108
furniture

**Foster Brothers
Manufacturing Company**
2025 South Vandeventer
St. Louis, MO 63110
wood products

Furniture Dynamics, Inc.
P.O. Box 426
Richardson, TX 75080
furniture

Game-Time, Inc.
980 Anderson Road
Litchfield, MI 49252
play equipment

Garret Wade
302 Fifth Avenue
New York, NY 10001
furniture

Georgia-Pacific Corporation
133 Peachtree Street NE
Atlanta, GA 30303
wood products

Gold Medal, Inc.
1700 Packard Avenue
Racine, WI 53403
furniture

Kenmore Industries, Inc.
Woodbine Road
P.O. Box 155
Belmont, MA 02178
wood products

Leichtung, Inc.
701 Beta Drive, No. 17
Cleveland, OH 44173
furniture

Loftcraft
1021 Third Avenue
New York, NY 10021
furniture

Louisiana-Pacific Corporation
1300 SW Fifth Avenue
Portland, OR 97204
trade association

Herman Miller, Inc.
600 Madison Avenue
New York, NY 10022
furniture

National Plan Service
435 West Fullerton Avenue
Elmhurst, IL 60126
wood project designs

Parrot Industries
44 Arco Place
Baltimore, MD 21227
wood products

Period, Inc.
P.O. Box 578
Henderson, KY 42420
furniture

Rojan Manufacturing Company
414 North 13th Street
Philadelphia, PA 19108
furniture, wood products

Romweber
4 South Park Avenue
Batesville, IN 47006
furniture

Scandinavian Design, Inc.
117 East 59th Street
New York, NY 10022
furniture

Southern Forest Products Association
P.O. Box 52468
New Orleans, LA 70152
trade association

Swan Brass Beds
1955 East 16th Street
Los Angeles, CA 90021
furniture

Thomasville Furniture Industries
P.O. Box 339
Thomasville, NC 27360
furniture

William J.B. Waite, Inc.
200 Kansas Street
San Francisco, CA 94103
furniture

Heywood Wakefield Company
206 Central Street
Gardner, MA 01440
furniture

Western Wood Products Association
1500 Yeon Building
Portland, OR 97204
trade association

West Michigan Furniture Company
195 West 8th Street
Holland, MI 49423
furniture

Woodcraft Supply Company
313 Montvale Avenue
Woburn, MA 01801
wood products

Index